contents

dazzling dressings…

Even a simple green salad becomes a treat when tossed with a well-flavoured dressing. Here are some of the classic dressings – if you prefer, you can blend or process them – or use a hand blender – rather than shake them in a jar. This gives the dressings a slightly thicker, creamier consistency.

thousand island dressing

1 cup (250ml) mayonnaise
¼ cup (60ml) tomato paste
¼ cup (60ml) tomato sauce
2 teaspoons worcestershire sauce
½ teaspoon tabasco sauce

Combine ingredients in small bowl; whisk until smooth. Cover and refrigerate until required.

makes about 1½ cups (375ml)

honey dijon dressing

¼ cup (60ml) honey
2 tablespoons dijon mustard
½ cup (125ml) white wine vinegar
1 tablespoon lemon juice
1 cup (250ml) groundnut oil

Combine honey, mustard, vinegar and juice in small bowl. Gradually whisk in oil; continue to whisk until dressing is slightly thickened and smooth.

makes about ⅔ cup (160ml)

dressings from left: Honey Dijon, French (see recipe page 5), Italian (see recipe page 5), Thousand Island

guilt-free dressing

½ cup buttermilk
2 tablespoons finely chopped
    fresh chives
2 tablespoons no-oil French dressing
1 tablespoon mustard
1 tablespoon honey

Combine ingredients in screw-top jar;
shake well.

makes about ⅔ cup (160ml)
per tablespoon 0.4g fat; 944kJ
(225 cal)

italian dressing

2 tablespoons white wine vinegar
2 tablespoons lemon juice
½ teaspoon sugar
2 cloves garlic, crushed
¾ cup (180ml) olive oil
1 tablespoon finely chopped
    fresh basil leaves
1 tablespoon finely chopped
    fresh oregano leaves

Combine ingredients in screw-top jar;
shake well.

makes about 1 cup (250ml)
per tablespoon 14.3g fat; 538kJ
(128 cal)

*clockwise from top left: Guilt-free,
French, Fresh Tomato and Italian*

french dressing

¼ cup (60ml) white vinegar
¾ cup (180ml) olive oil
½ teaspoon sugar
1 teaspoon dijon mustard

Combine ingredients in screw-top jar;
shake well.

makes about 1 cup (250ml)
per tablespoon 14.3g fat; 535kJ
(128 cal)

fresh tomato dressing

3 large (270g) plum tomatoes,
    peeled, deseeded, quartered
2 spring onions, chopped coarsely
⅓ cup (80ml) red wine vinegar
⅓ cup (80ml) sweet chilli sauce
2 cloves garlic, quartered
1 teaspoon mustard
1 teaspoon sugar
1 teaspoon cracked black pepper
¼ cup coarsely chopped fresh parsley

Blend or process ingredients until
almost smooth.

makes about 1¼ cups (310ml)
per tablespoon 0.2g fat; 45kJ
(11 cal)

... and mayonnaise

Mayonnaise is traditionally made using a bowl and whisk, adding the oil drop by drop at first, then in a thin stream. However, if you're in a hurry, a blender or food processor is faster. This method makes a much thicker sauce, which can be thinned with a little milk or water.

basic mayonnaise

2 egg yolks
1 tablespoon lemon juice
½ teaspoon salt
½ teaspoon mustard powder
½ cup (125ml) light olive oil
¼ cup (125ml) olive oil

1 Whisk, blend or process egg yolks, juice, salt and mustard until smooth.
2 Add combined oils gradually in thin stream while motor is operating; blend until thick.

makes about ¾ cup (180ml)
per tablespoon 27.7g fat; 1040kJ (248 cal)

thousand island mayonnaise

Whisk ⅓ cup (80ml) tomato paste, ⅓ cup (80ml) tomato sauce, 1 tablespoon worcestershire sauce, ½ teaspoon tabasco sauce, into ¾ cup (180ml) basic mayonnaise.

makes about 1¼ cups (310ml)
per tablespoon 16.7g fat; 668kJ (160 cal)

curried mayonnaise

Add 1 tablespoon curry powder to dry pan, stir over heat until fragrant; cool. Whisk into ¾ cup (180ml) mayonnaise.

makes about ¾ cup (180ml)
per tablespoon 27.9g fat; 1054kJ (252 cal)

herb mayonnaise

Whisk 2 tablespoons chopped chives, 2 tablespoons chopped parsley, 2 tablespoons chopped basil into ¾ cup (180ml) basic mayonnaise.

makes about ¾ cup (180ml)
per tablespoon 27.7g fat; 1041kJ (249 cal)

garlic mayonnaise

Follow the basic recipe, adding 3 crushed cloves garlic at stage 1.

makes about ¾ cup (180ml)
per tablespoon 27.7g fat; 1044kJ (249 cal)

clockwise from top left: Thousand Island, Curried, Garlic and Herb

marinades

Marinades not only infuse your meat and fish with the most delicious flavours, but they have the added benefit of making them more tender as well. Each of these recipes takes just 5 minutes to prepare and is sufficient for about 1kg of meat or fish. They can be made up to 3 days ahead if kept covered in the refrigerator, except for the yogurt marinade, which should be only prepared 1 day before using.

balsamic vinegar marinade

¼ cup (60ml) lemon juice
2 tablespoons olive oil
¼ cup (60ml) balsamic vinegar
2 cloves garlic, crushed
3 teaspoons brown sugar
2 teaspoons finely chopped thyme

Combine ingredients in medium jug.

makes ¾ cup
per quantity 36.7g fat; 1623kJ (388 cal)

red wine marinade

½ cup (125ml) dry red wine
2 teaspoons dijon mustard
1 clove garlic, crushed
½ teaspoon finely chopped thyme

Combine ingredients in medium jug.

makes ½ cup
per quantity 0.3g fat; 382kJ (91 cal)

clockwise from top left: Balsamic Vinegar, Honey Soy, Yogurt and Red Wine

honey soy marinade

1 tablespoon honey, warmed
⅓ cup (80ml) soy sauce
1 teaspoon sesame oil
2 cloves garlic, crushed
2 teaspoons grated fresh ginger

Combine ingredients in small jug.

makes ½ cup
per quantity 4.8g fat; 710kJ (170 cal)

yogurt marinade

½ cup (140g) plain yogurt
1 clove garlic, crushed
1 fresh red thai chilli, deseeded, chopped finely
½ teaspoon sweet paprika
2 teaspoons finely chopped fresh mint

Combine ingredients in small bowl.

makes ½ cup
per quantity 5g fat; 451kJ (108 cal)

9

paprika chicken with raisin & coriander pilaf

8 skinless chicken thigh cutlets (1.3kg)
2 tablespoons lemon juice
3 cloves garlic, crushed
½ teaspoon hot paprika
1 teaspoon sweet paprika
1 teaspoon ground cinnamon
¾ cup (200g) plain yogurt
1 tablespoon olive oil
1 medium brown onion (150g), chopped finely
2 cups (200g) basmati rice
1 litre (4 cups) chicken stock
½ cup (85g) chopped raisins
¾ cup chopped fresh coriander

1 Combine chicken, juice, garlic and spices in large bowl, cover; refrigerate 3 hours or overnight.
2 Cook chicken, in batches, on heated oiled grill plate or barbecue, brushing with a little of the yogurt, until browned and cooked through.
3 Meanwhile, heat oil in medium saucepan; cook onion, stirring, until softened. Add rice; stir to coat in onion mixture. Add stock; bring to a boil. Reduce heat; simmer, covered, stirring occasionally, about 25 minutes or until rice is almost tender. Stir in raisins; cook, covered, 5 minutes.
4 Stir coriander into pilaf off the heat just before serving. Top pilaf with chicken and remaining yogurt.

serves 4
per serving 11g fat; 2629kJ (629 cal)

11

tandoori chicken salad

½ cup (140g) plain yogurt
1½ tablespoons tandoori paste
750g chicken tenderloins
¾ cup (200g) plain yogurt, extra
¼ cup (60ml) mint sauce
250g mixed salad leaves
4 large plum tomatoes (360g), chopped
1 cucumber (260g), chopped

1 Combine yogurt and paste in large bowl, add chicken; stir until combined. Cover; marinate in refrigerator 3 hours.
2 Cook chicken, in batches, on heated oiled grill plate (or grill or barbecue) until browned on both sides and cooked through.
3 Meanwhile, combine extra yogurt and sauce in small bowl.
4 Divide salad leaves among serving plates, top with tomato, cucumber and chicken. Serve drizzled with yogurt mint sauce.

serves 4
per serving 14.8g fat; 1545kJ (369 cal)

soy chicken & spring-onion omelette salad

700g chicken breast fillets
2 tablespoons soy sauce
1 clove garlic, crushed
1 tablespoon groundnut oil
6 eggs
4 spring onions, sliced thinly
50g tat soi leaves
50g watercress

chilli dressing

1 tablespoon sweet chilli sauce
2 tablespoons lime juice
2 red thai chillies, chopped finely
¼ cup (60ml) groundnut oil
1 tablespoon sugar

1 Combine chicken, soy and garlic in large bowl; cover, refrigerate 3 hours or overnight.

2 Drain chicken; discard marinade. Heat oil in large pan; cook chicken, in batches, until browned all over and cooked through. Cover chicken; rest 5 minutes, slice thinly.

3 Meanwhile, whisk eggs in medium bowl with onion. Pour half of egg mixture into heated large non-stick pan; cook, tilting pan, over medium heat until egg mixture is almost set. Turn, cook further 2 minutes. Repeat with remaining mixture.

4 Roll omelettes together; cut into thin slices.

5 Gently toss chicken and omelette in large bowl with tat soi, watercress and three-quarters of the dressing. Serve remaining dressing separately.

chilli dressing Combine ingredients in screw-top jar; shake well.

serves 4
per serving 31.6g fat; 2034kJ (486 cal)

thai basil chicken stir-fry

1 teaspoon sesame oil

½ cup (125ml) light soy sauce

¼ cup (90g) honey

¼ cup (60ml) lime juice

3 fresh red thai chillies, deseeded, sliced thinly

2 teaspoons cornflour

850g chicken breast fillets, sliced thinly

2 tablespoons groundnut oil

3 cloves garlic, crushed

2 large red onions (600g), sliced thinly

240g fresh baby corn

2 teaspoons finely grated lime rind

3 cups (240g) beansprouts

2 cups loosely packed fresh thai basil leaves

1 cup loosely packed fresh coriander leaves

1 Combine sesame oil, sauce, honey, juice, chilli and cornflour in large bowl. Add chicken; toss to coat in marinade. Cover; refrigerate 3 hours or overnight.

2 Drain chicken over medium bowl; reserve marinade.

3 Heat half of the groundnut oil in wok or large non-stick frying pan; stir-fry chicken, in batches, until browned all over. Heat remaining groundnut oil in wok; stir-fry garlic, onion and corn until just tender. Return chicken to wok with reserved marinade and rind; stir-fry until sauce boils and chicken is cooked through.

4 Remove from heat; add beansprouts, basil and coriander. Toss with chicken and vegetables until combined. Serve with steamed jasmine rice and wedges of fresh lime, if desired.

serves 8

per serving 11.5g fat; 1219kJ (292 cal)

tip Grate rind from lime before juicing it.

chicken wings & green mango salad

10cm stick (20g) fresh lemongrass, chopped finely
1 fresh long green chilli, chopped finely
3 cloves garlic, crushed
10 fresh kaffir lime leaves, shredded finely
16 chicken wings (1.5kg)
2 small green mangoes (600g)
1 large carrot (180g)
½ cucumber (130g)
1 medium red pepper (200g), sliced thinly
2 spring onions, sliced thinly

sweet and sour dressing

2 tablespoons fish sauce
2 tablespoons lime juice
2 tablespoons grated palm sugar
1 tablespoon white vinegar
1 tablespoon water

1 Make sweet and sour dressing.
2 Combine lemongrass, chilli, garlic, half of the lime leaves and 2 tablespoons of the dressing in medium bowl, add chicken; toss chicken to coat in marinade. Cover remaining dressing and chicken separately; refrigerate 3 hours or overnight.
3 Drain chicken; discard marinade. Cook chicken on heated oiled grill plate, uncovered, until cooked through.
4 Meanwhile, use vegetable peeler to finely slice mangoes, carrot and cucumber into ribbons. Place in medium bowl with pepper, remaining lime leaves and remaining dressing; toss gently to combine. Serve chicken with salad, sprinkled with onion.

sweet and sour dressing Place ingredients in screw-top jar; shake well.

serves 4
per serving 13g fat; 1877kJ (449 cal)

marinated lamb salad with lemon yogurt dressing

750g lamb fillet
2 cloves garlic, crushed
1 tablespoon finely chopped
 fresh mint leaves
1 tablespoon finely shredded
 lemon rind
2 tablespoons lemon juice
2 medium (400g) red peppers
1 cucumber, sliced thinly
1 medium (170g) red onion,
 sliced thinly
100g kalamata olives, deseeded
100g feta cheese, crumbled
1 baby cos lettuce

lemon yogurt dressing
200ml natural yogurt
¼ cup (60ml) lemon juice
1 clove garlic, crushed
2 tablespoons water

1 Combine lamb with garlic, mint, rind and juice in large shallow dish; cover, refrigerate 3 hours or overnight.
2 Drain lamb; discard marinade. Cook lamb in heated oiled grill pan (or on grill or barbecue) until browned all over and cooked as desired. Cover lamb, rest 5 minutes; slice thinly.
3 Cut peppers into diamond shapes.
4 Gently toss lamb, pepper, cucumber, onion, olives, cheese and lettuce leaves in large bowl with dressing.

lemon yogurt dressing Whisk ingredients together in small bowl.

serves 4
per serving 52.8g fat; 2865kJ (684 cal)

spiced lamb salad with mango dressing

750g lamb eye of loin
1 tablespoon ground cumin
1 tablespoon ground coriander
2 teaspoons ground turmeric
½ teaspoon hot paprika
2 teaspoons garlic salt
2 tortilla wraps
1 (200g) red pepper, sliced thinly
1 (200g) yellow pepper, sliced thinly
1 (170g) red onion, sliced thinly
2 (500g) avocados, sliced thinly
1 round lettuce, trimmed
2 tablespoons fresh coriander

mango dressing

1 cup (250ml) mango puree
½ cup (125ml) lime juice

1 Place lamb in large bowl with combined spices and salt, cover; refrigerate 3 hours or overnight.
2 Cook lamb, uncovered, in heated oiled pan until browned all over and cooked as desired. Cover, rest 5 minutes; slice thinly.
3 Meanwhile, place wraps on oiled oven tray, bake, uncovered, in moderate oven about 5 minutes or until lightly browned. Cool; break into large pieces.
4 Divide lamb, peppers, onion, avocado, lettuce and coriander among serving plates; drizzle with dressing. Serve with wraps.

mango dressing Combine ingredients in screw-top jar; shake well.

serves 4
per serving 27.9g fat; 2417kJ (577 cal)
tip You will need about 2 small fresh mangoes (or drained, canned mango slices) for the puree in this recipe.

spicy braised lamb & yogurt

1 medium brown onion (150g),
   chopped coarsely
1 tablespoon grated fresh ginger
2 cloves garlic, crushed
1 teaspoon coriander seeds
1 teaspoon cumin seeds
½ teaspoon cardamom seeds
2 tablespoons lime juice
2.5kg leg of lamb, boned,
   chopped coarsely
30g ghee
¼ teaspoon cayenne pepper
2 teaspoons ground turmeric
1 teaspoon garam masala
⅔ cup (190g) natural yogurt
⅔ cup (160ml) double cream
1 cup (250ml) water
400g can chickpeas, rinsed,
   drained
2 medium tomatoes (380g),
   chopped coarsely
1 tablespoon plain flour
2 tablespoons water, extra
¼ cup chopped fresh flat-leaf
   parsley

1 Blend or process onion, ginger, garlic, seeds and juice until well combined. Place blended mixture and lamb in medium bowl; stir until lamb is well coated. Cover; marinate in refrigerator 3 hours or overnight.

2 Heat ghee in large saucepan; add cayenne pepper, turmeric and garam masala; stir over medium heat 1 minute.

3 Stir in yogurt, then lamb; stir over high heat until lamb is well browned. Stir in combined cream and water; bring to a boil. Reduce heat; simmer, uncovered, about 1 hour or until lamb is tender. Stir in chickpeas and tomato.

4 Stir in blended flour and the extra water; stir over high heat until sauce boils and thickens. Stir in parsley; serve with lime wedges, if desired.

serves 6
per serving 37.5g fat; 2877kJ (687 cal)
tips Ask your butcher to bone the leg of lamb for you.
Recipe can be made a day ahead and refrigerated, covered.

lamb with chermoulla

2 tablespoons grated lemon rind
2 cloves garlic, chopped coarsely
2 small fresh red chillies, deseeded, chopped coarsely
1 tablespoon grated fresh ginger
¼ cup chopped fresh flat-leaf parsley
¼ cup chopped fresh coriander
1 teaspoon sweet paprika
¼ cup (60ml) olive oil
8 lamb forequarter chops (1.5kg)

1 Blend or process rind, garlic, chilli, ginger, herbs, paprika and oil until well combined. Place lamb in single layer in shallow dish; coat lamb in chermoulla paste. Cover; refrigerate 3 hours or overnight.
2 Cook lamb, in batches, on heated oiled grill plate or barbecue until browned and cooked as desired. Serve with a mixed salad and lemon wedges, if desired.

serves 4
per serving 30.4g fat; 2103kJ (503 cal)

balsamic & rosemary lamb

2 tablespoons olive oil
¼ cup (60ml) balsamic vinegar
1 tablespoon fresh rosemary leaves
12 lamb cutlets (780g)

1 Combine oil, vinegar and rosemary in medium bowl, add lamb; toss
lamb to coat in marinade; cover, refrigerate 3 hours or overnight.
2 Drain lamb; discard marinade. Cook lamb on heated oiled grill plate,
uncovered, until cooked as desired.

serves 4
per serving 17.7g fat; 1007kJ (241 cal)

citrus-flavoured beef fillet with belgian endive

500g beef fillet
½ cup (135g) marmalade
½ cup (125ml) orange juice
2 tablespoons brown sugar
1 clove garlic, crushed
2 medium (480g) oranges
2 tablespoons groundnut oil
½ cup (80g) blanched almonds
2 spring onions, sliced thinly
1kg Belgian endive, leaves separated
¼ cup (60ml) orange juice, extra

1 Cut beef into thin slices; combine in large bowl with marmalade, juice, sugar and garlic. Cover; refrigerate 3 hours or overnight.
2 Drain beef over medium bowl; reserve marinade. Remove peel, pith and seeds from oranges; cut into 1cm-thick slices.
3 Heat the oil in wok or large pan; cook nuts, stirring, until just brown. Remove from wok to large bowl.
4 Add beef, in batches, to wok; stir-fry until just browned. Place in bowl along with nuts.
5 Add orange slices to same wok; cook, in batches, until just browned both sides. Place in bowl with nuts and beef, add onion; toss gently to combine.
6 Add reserved marinade to wok, bring to boil; boil 1 minute.
7 Divide endive among serving plates; top with beef salad, drizzle with combined cooled marinade and extra juice.

serves 4
per serving 28.9g fat; 2698kJ (644 cal)
tip Beef will be easier to slice if it has been wrapped tightly in cling film and placed in the freezer for an hour or so.
You can use the red or white variety of endive (or even its near-cousin, radicchio) for this recipe.

balsamic & ginger beef

½ cup (125ml) olive oil
¼ cup (60ml) balsamic vinegar
1 tablespoon grated fresh ginger
1 teaspoon brown sugar
1 teaspoon soy sauce
4 beef T-bone steaks (1kg)

1 Combine oil, vinegar, ginger, sugar and sauce in screw-top jar; shake well. Reserve ¼ cup (60ml) of the vinegar mixture; brush beef all over using about half of the remaining mixture. Cover; refrigerate 3 hours or overnight.
2 Cook beef under heated grill until browned and cooked as desired, brushing beef occasionally with remaining vinegar mixture during cooking.
3 Pour reserved vinegar mixture over beef. Serve with salad.

serves 4
per serving 37.3g fat; 1967kJ (470 cal)

veal t-bones with chickpea & tomato salad

4 veal T-bone steaks (750g)
1 teaspoon ground coriander
1 teaspoon ground cumin
¼ teaspoon chilli powder
2 teaspoons grated lemon rind
1 tablespoon olive oil

chickpea and tomato salad

300g can chickpeas, drained
2 large tomatoes (500g), deseeded, chopped
1 small red onion (100g), chopped
2 spring onions, chopped finely
2 tablespoons chopped fresh coriander
1 tablespoon chopped fresh mint
1 teaspoon grated lemon rind
¼ cup (60ml) lemon juice
⅓ cup (80ml) olive oil

1 Combine veal, spices, chilli, rind and oil in large bowl; cover, refrigerate 3 hours or overnight.
2 Cook veal, in batches, on heated oiled grill plate or barbecue until browned and cooked as desired.
3 Serve veal with chickpea and tomato salad.

chickpea and tomato salad Combine salad ingredients in a serving bowl.

serves 4
per serving 28.9g fat; 1956kJ (468 cal)

thai beef salad

¼ cup (60ml) fish sauce
¼ cup (60ml) lime juice
500g beef rump steak
1 large cucumber (390g), deseeded, sliced thinly
4 fresh small red thai chillies, sliced thinly
4 spring onions, sliced thinly
250g cherry tomatoes, halved
¼ cup firmly packed fresh vietnamese mint leaves
½ cup firmly packed fresh coriander leaves
½ cup firmly packed fresh thai basil leaves
1 tablespoon grated palm sugar
2 teaspoons soy sauce
1 clove garlic, crushed

1 Combine 2 tablespoons of the fish sauce and 1 tablespoon of the juice in medium bowl, add beef; toss beef to coat in marinade. Cover; refrigerate 3 hours or overnight.
2 Drain beef; discard marinade. Cook beef on heated oiled grill plate (or grill or barbecue) until cooked as desired. Cover beef, stand 5 minutes; slice beef thinly.
3 Meanwhile, combine cucumber, chilli, onion, tomato and herbs in large bowl.
4 Place sugar, soy sauce, garlic, remaining fish sauce and remaining juice in screw-top jar; shake well. Add beef and dressing to salad; toss gently to combine.

serves 4
per serving 8.7g fat; 982kJ (235 cal)

beef & asparagus salad with mustard-seed dressing

500g beef fillet
¾ cup (180ml) dry red wine
2 cloves garlic, crushed
500g fresh asparagus, trimmed
500g chestnut mushrooms
120g thinly sliced pancetta
300g mangetout
1 red mignonette lettuce

mustard-seed dressing
⅓ cup (80ml) red wine vinegar
2 teaspoons mustard
¼ cup (60ml) mustard-seed oil
¼ cup (60ml) olive oil

1 Cut beef crossways into four even-sized pieces; combine with wine and garlic in large bowl. Cover; refrigerate 3 hours or overnight.
2 Drain beef; discard marinade. Cook beef, in batches, on heated oiled grill plate (or grill or barbecue) until browned all over and cooked as desired. Cover beef; rest 5 minutes, slice thinly.
3 Wipe cooled grill plate clean with absorbent paper. Oil and reheat grill plate; cook asparagus, in batches, until browned and just tender. Cut asparagus into 5cm lengths.
4 Cook mushrooms, in batches, on same grill plate until brown and just tender.
5 Cook pancetta, in batches, on same grill plate until crisp; chop coarsely.
6 Halve mangetout diagonally; boil, steam or microwave until just tender. Drain; cool.
7 Gently toss beef, asparagus, mushroom, pancetta, mangetout and lettuce in large bowl with dressing.

mustard-seed dressing Combine ingredients in screw-top jar; shake well.

serves 4
per serving 36.3g fat; 2297kJ (549 cal)
tips Mustard-seed oil is a mild-tasting oil made from the first pressing of fine yellow mustard seeds. A nut oil such as macadamia or hazelnut can be used in place of the mustard-seed oil if you prefer.
You can substitute fresh shiitake or even button mushrooms for the chestnut mushrooms in this recipe if you like.

basil & oregano steak with char-grilled vegetables

2 teaspoons finely chopped fresh oregano

¼ cup finely chopped fresh basil

1 tablespoon finely grated lemon rind

2 tablespoons lemon juice

4 drained anchovy fillets, chopped finely

4 x 200g beef sirloin steaks

2 baby fennel bulbs (260g), quartered

3 small courgette (270g), chopped coarsely

1 large red pepper (350g), sliced thickly

200g portobello mushrooms, sliced thickly

4 baby aubergines (240g), chopped coarsely

2 small red onions (200g), sliced thickly

2 teaspoons olive oil

¼ cup (60ml) lemon juice, extra

2 tablespoons fresh oregano leaves

1 Combine chopped oregano, basil, rind, the 2 tablespoons of lemon juice and anchovy in large bowl, add beef; toss beef to coat in marinade. Cover; refrigerate 3 hours or overnight.

2 Meanwhile, combine fennel, courgette, pepper, mushroom, aubergine, onion and oil in large bowl; cook vegetables, in batches, on heated lightly oiled grill plate (or grill or barbecue) until just tender. Add extra juice and oregano leaves to bowl with vegetables; toss gently to combine. Cover to keep warm.

3 Cook beef mixture on same grill plate until cooked as desired; serve with the char-grilled vegetables.

serves 4

per serving 21.7g fat; 1823kJ (436 cal)

tandoori beef & dhal
with cucumber dressing

2 teaspoons ground turmeric
2 teaspoons ground cumin
2 teaspoons ground coriander
1 tablespoon sweet paprika
1 teaspoon garlic salt
¼ cup (60ml) groundnut oil
800g beef fillet
1 cup (200g) moong dhal (split
   mung beans)
150g green beans

2 red thai chillies, sliced thinly
1 medium (170g) red onion,
   chopped finely
1 tablespoon cumin seeds, toasted

cucumber dressing
½ cucumber
200ml natural yogurt
½ cup loosely packed fresh mint
1 tablespoon lemon juice

1 Combine spices, salt and the oil in large bowl. Add beef, coat with spice mixture, cover; refrigerate 3 hours or overnight.

2 Cook beef in heated large non-stick pan, uncovered, about 5 minutes or until browned all over. Place beef in baking dish; bake, uncovered, in moderate oven about 30 minutes or until cooked as desired. Cover beef; rest 10 minutes, slice thinly.

3 Meanwhile, add dhal to pan of boiling water; cook, uncovered, about 10 minutes or until just tender, stirring occasionally. Drain, cool.

4 Top and tail beans; cut into 3cm lengths. Boil, steam or microwave beans until just tender; rinse under cold water, drain.

5 Gently toss beef, dhal, beans, chilli, onion and cumin seeds in large bowl with dressing.

cucumber dressing Cut cucumber in half lengthways, discard seeds; chop coarsely. Blend or process cucumber and remaining ingredients until almost smooth.

serves 4
per serving 27.3g fat; 2302kJ (550 cal)
tips To toast cumin seeds, dry-fry in small pan, stirring until fragrant. Dressing is best made at least 3 hours ahead; keep, covered, in refrigerator. We didn't seed the chillies deliberately in this recipe, but do so by all means if you can't stand the heat!

chilli marinated beef in coconut curry sauce

1.5kg beef braising steak, chopped
  coarsely
40g ghee
2 medium red peppers (400g),
  chopped finely
2 medium brown onions (300g),
  chopped finely
½ cup (125ml) beef stock
½ cup (125ml) coconut milk
1 cinnamon stick
5 dried curry leaves
⅓ cup chopped fresh coriander

spicy marinade

⅓ cup (80ml) white vinegar
2 fresh red thai chillies, sliced thinly
2 tablespoons tomato paste
1 tablespoon chopped fresh
  coriander
2 cloves garlic, crushed
3 cardamom pods, crushed
2 teaspoons cumin seeds
1 teaspoon ground turmeric

1 Combine beef and marinade in large bowl; mix well. Cover; refrigerate 3 hours or overnight.
2 Heat half of the ghee in large pan; cook beef, in batches, stirring, until browned all over.
3 Heat remaining ghee in same pan; cook pepper and onion, stirring, until onion is soft.
4 Return beef to pan; add stock, coconut milk, cinnamon and curry leaves. Simmer, covered, 1 hour, stirring occasionally.
5 Remove cover; simmer about 30 minutes or until beef is tender. Discard cinnamon stick; stir in coriander.
6 Serve with steamed or boiled rice, if desired.

spicy marinade Combine ingredients in large bowl; mix well.

serves 6
per serving 23g fat; 1853kJ (443 cal)
tip Recipe can be made a day ahead and refrigerated, covered; suitable for freezing.

teriyaki pork
with wasabi dressing

750g pork fillets
¼ cup (60ml) teriyaki marinade
50g mangetout sprouts
100g mixed baby salad leaves
50g watercress, trimmed
1 medium red pepper (200g), sliced thinly
250g yellow cherry tomatoes, halved

wasabi dressing
1½ teaspoons wasabi powder
¼ cup (60ml) cider vinegar
⅓ cup (80ml) vegetable oil
1 tablespoon light soy sauce

1 Brush pork with teriyaki marinade. Cook pork, in batches, on heated oiled grill plate or barbecue, brushing frequently with marinade, until browned and cooked through; cover to keep warm.
2 Meanwhile, combine sprouts, salad leaves, watercress, pepper and tomato in large bowl.
3 Pour wasabi dressing over salad mixture; toss gently to combine. Slice pork; serve with salad.

wasabi dressing Blend wasabi powder with vinegar in small jug; whisk in remaining ingredients.

serves 4
per serving 23g fat; 1797kJ (430 cal)

warm pork & mandarin salad

500g pork fillet, sliced thinly
2 cloves garlic, crushed
1 teaspoon grated fresh ginger
1 tablespoon sweet chilli sauce
2 teaspoons soy sauce
3 small (300g) mandarins,
  segmented
150g sugar snap peas
2 tablespoons groundnut oil
300g curly endive, trimmed
¼ cup firmly packed fresh
  coriander leaves
1 small (100g) red onion, sliced
  thinly

chilli dressing

1 tablespoon white wine vinegar
1 tablespoon groundnut oil
1 tablespoon sweet chilli sauce
2 teaspoons soy sauce

1 Combine pork, garlic, ginger and sauces in small bowl, cover; refrigerate 2 hours or overnight.

2 Halve mandarin segments lengthways; discard seeds.

3 Boil, steam or microwave peas until just tender; drain.

4 Heat the oil in wok or large pan; stir-fry pork, in batches, until browned and cooked as desired. Gently toss pork, mandarin and peas in large bowl with endive, coriander, onion and dressing.

chilli dressing Combine ingredients in screw-top jar; shake well.

serves 4
per serving 25g fat; 1630kJ (389 cal)

gingered pork with vegetables

700g pork fillets, sliced thinly
2 tablespoons grated fresh ginger
¼ cup chopped fresh coriander
2 tablespoons rice vinegar
2 tablespoons groundnut oil
125g fresh baby corn, halved
   lengthways
1 medium red pepper (200g), sliced
   thinly
100g mangetout, halved
2 tablespoons light soy sauce
250g spinach, trimmed
3 cups (240g) beansprouts
½ cup fresh coriander leaves, extra

1 Combine pork in medium bowl with ginger, coriander and vinegar. Cover; marinate in refrigerator 3 hours or overnight.
2 Heat half of the oil in wok or large frying pan; stir-fry pork mixture, in batches, until pork is browned and cooked through.
3 Heat remaining oil in same wok. Stir-fry corn, pepper and mangetout until just tender; remove from wok. Return pork to wok with soy sauce; stir-fry until heated through. Just before serving, return cooked vegetables to wok and gently toss with pork, spinach, beansprouts and extra coriander until spinach just wilts.

serves 4
per serving 13.8g fat; 1443kJ (345 cal)

chinese marinated pork

1kg piece pork neck

chinese marinade
2 star anise, crushed
2 tablespoons light soy sauce
2 tablespoons brown sugar
1½ tablespoons honey
1½ tablespoons dry sherry
2 teaspoons hoisin sauce
2 teaspoons grated fresh ginger
1 clove garlic, crushed
2 spring onions, chopped finely
 few drops red food colouring

1 Cut pork into quarters lengthways. Combine pork and marinade in large shallow dish. Cover; refrigerate 3 hours or overnight.
2 Drain pork; reserve marinade.
3 Cook pork on heated oiled barbecue, uncovered, until browned and cooked through, brushing with reserved marinade during cooking.

chinese marinade Combine ingredients in small bowl.

serves 6
per serving 6.5g fat; 1051kJ (251 cal)

salsas

Originating in Mexico, salsa simply means 'sauce' and is a spicy blend of chopped vegetables and fruit, with added fresh herbs and spices.

mango & avocado salsa

Combine 1 coarsely chopped mango (430g), 1 large (320g) coarsely chopped avocado, 1 finely chopped small (100g) red onion, 1 finely chopped small (150g) red pepper, 1 finely chopped small fresh red chilli, and 2 tablespoons lime juice together in a medium bowl.

makes 2½ cups
per tablespoon 1.7g fat; 100kJ (24 cal)

salsa fresca

Combine ½ cup finely chopped flat-leaf parsley, ¼ cup finely chopped fresh dill, ¼ cup finely chopped fresh chives, 1 tablespoon wholegrain mustard, 2 tablespoons lemon juice, 2 tablespoons finely chopped drained, rinsed baby capers, 1 crushed clove garlic, ⅓ cup (80ml) olive oil together in a small bowl.

makes 1 cup
per tablespoon 6.1g fat; 242kJ (58 cal)

clockwise from top left: Mango & Avocado, Chargrilled Pepper & Green Olive, Black Bean and Salsa Fresca

chargrilled pepper & green olive salsa

Blend or process 1 cup (120g) pitted, chopped green olives until smooth. Stir in 150g chargrilled red pepper, 1 small (100g) finely chopped red onion, 1 tablespoon lime juice, ⅓ cup coarsely chopped fresh coriander and a further 1 cup (120g) pitted, chopped green olives.

makes 2 cups
per tablespoon 0.1g fat; 59kJ (14 cal)

black bean salsa

Cook ¾ cup (150g) dried black beans according to directions on packet. In a large bowl combine the beans with 2 medium red peppers (400g), roasted, peeled and thinly sliced, 2 cups frozen corn kernels, 1 small (100g) chopped red onion, 1 finely chopped fresh long red chilli, ⅓ cup coarsely chopped coriander, 2 crushed cloves garlic, 2 tablespoons olive oil, 1 tablespoon finely grated lime rind, ½ cup (125ml) lime juice and 1 teaspoon ground cumin.

makes 4 cups
per tablespoon 0.9g fat; 109kJ (26 cal)

prawn salad with gazpacho salsa

Saffron, the dried stigma from the crocus flower, is the world's costliest spice.
Buy it in small amounts and keep it, sealed tightly, in the refrigerator to preserve
its freshness.

1kg cooked king prawns
2 medium (500g) avocados

gazpacho salsa

1 cucumber, deseeded,
  chopped finely
2 medium (380g) tomatoes,
  deseeded, chopped finely
1 clove garlic, crushed
1 tablespoon olive oil
2 tablespoons tomato juice
1 tablespoon raspberry
  vinegar

saffron mayonnaise

2 tablespoons lemon juice
¼ teaspoon saffron threads
2 egg yolks
1 tablespoon dijon mustard
⅓ cup (80ml) olive oil
1 tablespoon finely chopped
  fresh dill
1 tablespoon warm water

1 Make salsa and mayonnaise, as directed below, first.
2 Shell and devein prawns, leaving tails and heads intact.
3 Halve avocados; discard seeds.
4 Divide three-quarters of the salsa among serving plates. Place avocado halves on top; fill avocado centres with remaining salsa and prawns, spoon mayonnaise over prawns.

gazpacho salsa Combine ingredients in medium bowl; mix well.

saffron mayonnaise Gently heat juice and saffron in small pan over low heat, about 2 minutes or until juice has changed colour; cool. Blend or process strained juice, egg yolks and mustard until smooth. With motor operating, gradually add oil in thin stream until combined. Stir in dill; add the water to thin mayonnaise, if desired.

serves 4
per serving 56.6g fat; 3163kJ (755 cal)
tip Saffron mayonnaise is even better if made a day ahead; keep, covered, in refrigerator.

cajun lamb cutlets with cucumber salsa

12 lamb cutlets (900g)
2 teaspoons ground cumin
2 teaspoons ground coriander
1 teaspoon ground turmeric
1 teaspoon sweet paprika
1 teaspoon ground oregano
1 teaspoon chilli powder
½ teaspoon ground cloves
2 tablespoons olive oil

cucumber salsa

1 cucumber (260g), deseeded, chopped
2 medium tomatoes (260g), deseeded, chopped
1 medium yellow pepper (200g), chopped
2 spring onions, chopped finely
1 tablespoon balsamic vinegar
1 tablespoon olive oil

1 Coat lamb with combined spices and oil in large bowl. Cover, refrigerate 3 hours or overnight.
2 Cook lamb, in batches, on heated oiled grill plate or barbecue until browned and cooked as desired. Serve lamb with cucumber salsa.

cucumber salsa Combine ingredients in small bowl, cover; refrigerate 30 minutes.

serves 4
per serving 28.4g fat; 1994kJ (477 cal)

cajun chicken with chunky salsa

4 chicken breast fillets (680g)
1 teaspoon cracked black pepper
2 tablespoons finely chopped
  fresh oregano
2 teaspoons sweet paprika
1 teaspoon dried chilli flakes
2 cloves garlic, crushed
2 teaspoons olive oil

chunky salsa

2 medium tomatoes (300g),
  chopped coarsely
1 small red onion (100g), chopped
  coarsely
1 medium green pepper (200g),
  chopped coarsely
2 tablespoons coarsely chopped
  fresh coriander
2 teaspoons olive oil
2 tablespoons lime juice

1 Place chicken in large bowl with combined remaining ingredients; toss chicken to coat in mixture. Cover; refrigerate 15 minutes.

2 Meanwhile, make chunky salsa.

3 Cook chicken in large lightly oiled non-stick frying pan until cooked through. Serve chicken with salsa.

chunky salsa Combine ingredients in medium bowl.

serves 4
per serving 8.7g fat; 1083kJ (259 cal)
tip Serve with warm corn tortillas, if desired.

pesto chicken with tomato salsa

1kg chicken tenderloins
¾ cup (195g) sun-dried tomato
 pesto

tomato salsa
4 medium tomatoes (760g)
6 spring onions, sliced thinly
1 medium red onion (170g),
 chopped finely
2 tablespoons lemon juice
1 tablespoon olive oil
½ teaspoon freshly ground black
 pepper

1 Trim chicken. Combine chicken
and pesto in large bowl. Cover;
marinate in refrigerator 3 hours or
overnight.
2 Preheat oven to hot. Place
chicken on wire rack over baking
dish; cook, uncovered, in hot oven
about 25 minutes or until chicken is
cooked and tender. Cool 5 minutes;
refrigerate until cold. Slice chicken
and serve with salsa.

tomato salsa Remove seeds from tomatoes; chop tomatoes finely. Combine
tomato with remaining ingredients in medium bowl.

serves 4
per serving 26g fat; 2142kJ (512 cal)
tip We used vine-ripened tomatoes in our salsa, however any variety of tomato
can be used.

pork & corn salsa tortilla wraps

600g pork fillet, sliced thinly
2 tablespoons vegetable oil
35g packet taco seasoning mix
16 small corn tortillas
1 round lettuce, torn
½ cup (120g) reduced-fat soured cream

corn salsa
310g can corn kernels, drained
3 medium tomatoes (450g), chopped coarsely
1 small red onion (100g), chopped finely
½ cup coarsely chopped fresh coriander

1 Combine pork, oil and taco seasoning mix in medium bowl.
2 Warm the tortillas according to directions on packet.
3 Cook pork on heated oiled grill plate or in large frying pan until pork is browned and cooked through.
4 Make the corn salsa.
5 Serve pork wrapped in tortillas with corn salsa, lettuce and soured cream.

corn salsa Combine corn, tomato, onion and coriander in medium bowl.

serves 4
per serving 23.9g fat; 3265kJ (781 cal)
tip This recipe can be prepared several hours ahead; cook and assemble just before serving.

beef fajitas with salsa cruda & avocado mash

2 tablespoons vegetable oil
⅓ cup (80ml) lime juice
¼ cup coarsely chopped fresh oregano
2 cloves garlic, crushed
¼ cup coarsely chopped fresh coriander
2 teaspoons ground cumin
800g beef rump steak
1 medium red pepper (200g), sliced thickly
1 medium green pepper (200g), sliced thickly
1 medium yellow pepper (200g), sliced thickly
1 large red onion (300g), sliced thickly
20 small flour tortillas

salsa cruda
2 cloves garlic, crushed
3 medium tomatoes (450g), deseeded, chopped finely
1 white onion (80g), chopped finely
2 trimmed radishes (30g), chopped finely
½ cucumber (130g), chopped finely
2 tablespoons coarsely chopped fresh coriander
1 fresh long red chilli, chopped finely
2 tablespoons lime juice

avocado mash
2 small avocados (400g)
2 tablespoons lime juice

1 Combine oil, juice, oregano, garlic, coriander and cumin in large bowl, add beef; toss beef to coat in marinade. Cover; refrigerate 3 hours or overnight.
2 Cook beef, peppers and onion on heated oiled flat plate, uncovered, until beef is cooked as desired and vegetables are just tender. Cover to keep warm.
3 Meanwhile, make salsa cruda and avocado mash. Warm tortillas according to directions on packet.
4 Cut beef into 1cm slices; combine with cooked vegetables in large bowl. Serve with salsa cruda, avocado mash and tortillas.

salsa cruda Combine ingredients in small bowl.

avocado mash Mash avocado and juice in small bowl.

serves 4
per serving 46.7g fat; 5229kJ (1251 cal)

tex-mex spareribs
with grilled corn salsa

2 tablespoons brown sugar
1 tablespoon dried oregano
2 tablespoons sweet paprika
2 teaspoons cracked black pepper
½ teaspoon cayenne pepper
1 tablespoon ground cumin
1 tablespoon garlic powder
¼ cup (60ml) water
2 tablespoons vegetable oil
1.5kg American-style pork spareribs

grilled corn salsa
3 trimmed corn cobs (750g)
2 medium tomatoes (300g), deseeded, chopped finely
1 fresh long green chilli, chopped finely
1 medium red onion (170g), chopped finely
1 medium green pepper (200g), chopped finely
¼ cup coarsely chopped fresh coriander
2 tablespoons lime juice
1 tablespoon olive oil

1 Combine sugar, oregano, spices, the water and oil in large bowl; add pork, rub spice mixture all over pork. Cook pork on heated oiled flat plate, uncovered, until cooked as desired.
2 Make the grilled corn salsa. Serve the pork with the grilled corn salsa.

grilled corn salsa Cook corn on heated oiled grill plate, uncovered, until tender. When cool enough to handle, cut kernels from cobs. Place kernels in medium bowl with remaining ingredients; toss salsa gently to combine.

serves 4
per serving 33.7g fat; 2445kJ (585 cal)

steaks with green pepper salsa

4 small beef fillet steaks (600g)

green pepper salsa
2 small green peppers (300g), chopped finely

1 small red onion (100g), chopped finely

1 medium red thai chilli, deseeded, chopped

6 spring onions, sliced

¼ cup (60ml) lime juice

2 tablespoons chopped fresh mint

1 Cook beef on heated oiled grill plate (or grill or barbecue) until browned on both sides and cooked as desired.
2 Serve beef with green pepper salsa and, if desired, baby spinach leaves.

green pepper salsa Combine ingredients in medium bowl.

serves 4
per serving 7.4g fat; 912kJ (218 cal)

fettuccini with rocket pesto & fresh tomato salsa

500g fettuccine
8 cloves garlic, quartered
½ cup loosely packed, chopped
    fresh basil
120g rocket, chopped coarsely
⅔ cup (160ml) olive oil
½ cup (40g) finely grated parmesan
    cheese
3 medium tomatoes (570g),
    chopped coarsely
2 tablespoons lemon juice
2 fresh red thai chillies, sliced thinly
⅓ cup (50g) pine nuts, toasted

1 Cook pasta in large pan of boiling water, uncovered, until just tender; drain.
2 Meanwhile, blend or process garlic, basil, rocket and oil until smooth.
3 Combine pasta, rocket pesto, cheese, tomato, juice and chilli in large saucepan; cook, stirring, until hot. Add nuts; toss gently to combine.

serves 4
per serving 50.3g fat; 3780kJ (904 cal)
tip Substitute baby spinach leaves for the rocket to give a milder-flavoured pesto.

salmon with
corn & pepper salsa

6 salmon fillets or cutlets (1.2kg)

corn & pepper salsa
2 trimmed corn cobs (500g)
2 medium red peppers (400g)
1 small red onion (100g), chopped finely
1 fresh red thai chilli, deseeded, chopped finely
1 tablespoon olive oil
¼ cup chopped fresh coriander

1 Cook salmon on heated oiled barbecue plate until browned both sides and cooked as desired. Salmon is best served a little rare in the centre.
2 Serve salmon with corn salsa and toasted bread, if desired.

corn & pepper salsa Cook corn on heated oiled barbecue plate, covered loosely with a piece of foil, about 20 minutes or until browned all over and tender. Using a sharp knife, cut kernels from cobs. Quarter peppers; remove and discard seeds and membranes. Cook on heated oiled barbecue plate until skin blisters and blackens. Cover pepper pieces with plastic or paper 5 minutes. Peel away and discard skin; chop pepper flesh finely. Combine corn, pepper, onion, chilli, oil and coriander in medium bowl.

serves 6
per serving 18.5g fat; 1766kJ (422 cal)
tips Barbecuing corn gives it a distinctive smoky flavour.
Corn & pepper salsa can be made 3 hours ahead.

glossary

black beans earthy-flavoured dried beans; mostly used in Mexican, South- and Central-American and the Caribbean cuisine.

buttermilk fresh low-fat milk cultured to give a slightly sour taste; low-fat yogurt or milk can be substituted.

cardamom can be bought in pod, seed or ground form. Has an aromatic, sweetly rich flavour.

cayenne pepper thin-fleshed, long, very-hot red chilli; usually purchased dried and ground.

chillies come in many types and sizes, fresh and dried. Wear rubber gloves when handling, as chillies can burn your skin. Removing seeds and membranes lessens the heat.

coriander

dried a fragrant herb, coriander seeds and ground coriander must never be used to replace fresh coriander or vice versa. The tastes are completely different.

fresh bright-green-leafed herb with a pungent flavour.

cumin available both ground and as whole seeds; cumin has a warm, earthy, rather strong flavour.

curry leaves bright-green, shiny, sharp-ended leaves with a flavour similar to curry powder, hence their name; are used fresh or dried.

feta cheese a crumbly goat's or sheep's milk cheese with a sharp salty taste.

fish sauce made from pulverised salted fermented fish, mostly anchovies. Has a pungent smell and strong taste; use sparingly.

garam masala a blend of spices based on roasted cardamom, cinnamon, cloves, coriander, fennel and cumin.

ghee a pure butter fat available in cans; can be heated to high temperatures without burning due to its lack of salt and milk solids.

ginger the thick gnarled root of a tropical plant.

groundnut oil oil pressed from ground peanuts; most commonly used in Asian cooking because of its high smoke point.

herbs use dried (not ground) herbs in the proportion of 1:4 for fresh herbs, eg. 1 teaspoon dried herbs for teaspoons chopped fresh herbs.

kaffir lime leaves aromatic leaves used fresh or dried in Asian dishes.

lemongrass a tall, lemon-smelling and tasting, sharp edged grass; use only the white lower part of the stem.

mustard

powder finely ground white (yellow) mustard seeds.

dijon a pale brown, distinctively flavoured fairly mild French mustard.

wholegrain a French-style coarse-grain mustard made from crushed mustard seeds and French mustard.

mustard-seed oil a mild-tasting oil made from yellow mustard seeds; macadamia or hazelnut oil can be used instead.

palm sugar made from the sap of the sugar palm tree. Light brown to black in colour and usually sold in rock-hard cakes. Substitute brown sugar, if preferred.

pancetta Italian unsmoked cured pork belly; bacon can be substituted.

paprika ground dried red pepper; available sweet, hot or smoked.

pine nuts small, cream-coloured kernels obtained from the cones of different varieties of pine trees.

saffron stigma of a member of crocus family, available in strands or ground form; imparts a yellow-orange colour to food. Quality varies – the best is the most expensive spice in the world. Store in freezer.

sesame oil made from roasted, crushed, white sesame seeds; for flavouring rather than cooking.

soy sauce made from fermented soy beans; several varieties are available.

sweet chilli sauce mild, Thai sauce made from red chillies, sugar, garlic and vinegar.

tabasco brand name of an extremely fiery sauce made from vinegar, hot red peppers and salt.

taco seasoning a packaged seasoning mix of oregano, cumin, chillies and various other spices.

tandoori paste Indian blend of hot and fragrant spices including turmeric, paprika, chilli powder, saffron, cardamom and garam masala.

teriyaki a sauce made from soy sauce, corn syrup, vinegar, ginger and other spices; a distinctive glaze on grilled meats.

thai basil different from sweet basil in both look and taste, having smaller leaves and purplish stems. It has a slight aniseed taste and is available from Asian food stores.

turmeric has a somewhat acrid aroma and pungent flavour. Known for the golden colour it gives dishes.

vietnamese mint a pungent and peppery narrow-leafed member of the buckwheat family. A common ingredient in Asian foods, particularly soups, salads and stir-fries.

vinegar

balsamic made from an Italian wine of white trebbiano grapes aged in antique wooden casks to give the exquisite pungent flavour.

cider made from fermented apples.

raspberry made from raspberries steeped in a white wine vinegar.

red wine based on fermented red wine.

rice wine made from rice wine lees (sediment), salt and alcohol.

white made from cane sugar spirit.

white wine based on fermented white wine.

wasabi asian horseradish used to make pungent, green sauce served with Japanese raw fish dishes; sold in powder or paste form.

worcestershire sauce a thin, dark-brown spicy sauce.

conversion charts

MEASURES

The cup and spoon measurements used in this book are metric: one measuring cup holds approximately 250ml; one metric tablespoon holds 20ml; one metric teaspoon holds 5ml.

All cup and spoon measurements are level.

The most accurate way of measuring dry ingredients is to weigh them. When measuring liquids, use a clear glass or plastic jug with metric markings.

We use large eggs with an average weight of 60g.

warning This book may contain recipes for dishes made with raw or lightly cooked eggs. These should be avoided by vulnerable people such as pregnant and nursing mothers, invalids, the elderly, babies and young children.

DRY MEASURES

METRIC	IMPERIAL
15g	½oz
30g	1oz
60g	2oz
90g	3oz
125g	4oz (¼lb)
155g	5oz
185g	6oz
220g	7oz
250g	8oz (½lb)
280g	9oz
315g	10oz
345g	11oz
375g	12oz (¾lb)
410g	13oz
440g	14oz
470g	15oz
500g	16oz (1lb)
750g	24oz (1½lb)
1kg	32oz (2lb)

LIQUID MEASURES

METRIC	IMPERIAL
30ml	1 fl oz
60ml	2 fl oz
100ml	3 fl oz
125ml	4 fl oz
150ml	5 fl oz (¼ pint/1 gill)
190ml	6 fl oz
250ml	8 fl oz
300ml	10 fl oz (½ pint)
500ml	16 fl oz
600ml	20 fl oz (1 pint)
1000ml (1 litre)	1¾ pints

LENGTH MEASURES

METRIC	IMPERIAL
3mm	⅛in
6mm	¼in
1cm	½in
2cm	¾in
2.5cm	1in
5cm	2in
6cm	2½in
8cm	3in
10cm	4in
13cm	5in
15cm	6in
18cm	7in
20cm	8in
23cm	9in
25cm	10in
28cm	11in
30cm	12in (1ft)

OVEN TEMPERATURES

These oven temperatures are only a guide for conventional ovens.
For fan-assisted ovens, check the manufacturer's manual.

	°C (CELSIUS)	°F (FAHRENHEIT)	GAS MARK
Very low	120	250	½
Low	150	275–300	1–2
Moderately low	160	325	3
Moderate	180	350–375	4–5
Moderately hot	200	400	6
Hot	220	425–450	7–8
Very hot	240	475	9

index